Combine Harvesters

Hannah Wilson

KINGFISHER
NEW YORK

KINGFISHER
LONDON & NEW YORK

First published 2015 by Kingfisher
Copyright © Macmillan Children's Books 2015
Published in the United States by Kingfisher,
175 Fifth Ave., New York, NY 10010
Kingfisher is an imprint of Macmillan Children's Books, London.

Distributed in the U.S. and Canada by Macmillan,
175 Fifth Ave., New York, NY 10010

Library of Congress Cataloging-in-Publication data
has been applied for

Series editor: Thea Feldman
Literacy consultant: Ellie Costa, Bank Street School for Children, New York

ISBN 978-0-7534-7221-7 (HB)
ISBN 978-0-7534-7222-4 (PB)

Kingfisher books are available for special promotions
and premiums. For details contact: Special Markets
Department, Macmillan, 175 Fifth Ave., New York, NY 10010.

For more information please visit
www.kingfisherbooks.com

Printed in China
9 8 7 6 5 4 3 2 1
1TR/0315/WKT/UG/115MA

Picture credits
The Publisher would like to thank the following for permission to reproduce their material.
Every care has been taken to trace copyright holders.
Top = t; Bottom = b; Center = c; Left = l; Right = r
Cover Shutterstock/smereka; 4 Shutterstock/My Portfolio; 5t Shutterstock/Svitlana-ua; 5b Shutterstock/
Pefkos; 6 Shutterstock/vladimir salman; 7 Shutterstock/Leonid Ikan; 8–9 Shutterstock/Ratikova;
8t Shutterstock/Perutskyi Petro; 9t Shutterstock/Kletr; 10–11 KF Archive; 12–13 Shutterstock/mihalec;
14l Shutterstock/Pefkos; 14–15 KF Archive; 15t Shutterstock/Ruud Morijn Photographer; 16 Shutterstock/
muratart; 17t Corbis/Christophe DI PASCALE/Photononstop; 17b Shutterstock/TwilightArtPictures;
18–19 Shutterstock/abdulrazak; 19t Shutterstock/Bullwinkle; 20 Getty/Roelof Bos; 21t Getty/Kevin Day;
21b Superstock/Design Pics; 22t Shutterstock/vladimir salman; 22m Shutterstock/Leonid Ikan; 22b
Shutterstock/mihalec; 23t Shutterstock/Pefkos; 23m Shutterstock/muratart; 23bl Corbis/Christophe DI
PASCALE/Photononstop; 24 Corbis/Bettmann; 25t Wisconsin History; 25b Wisconsin History; 26 Corbis/
© Lucas Schifres/Visuals Unlimited; 27 Shutterstock/surachet khamsuk; 28–29 CLAAS KGaA mbH; 29t with
the kind permission of Francis Godé; 30–31 Flickr/Russfeld.

Contents

A big machine

This big farm machine is called a combine harvester.

A combine harvester **harvests** the plants that grow on a farm.

Plants that grow on a farm
are called **crops**.

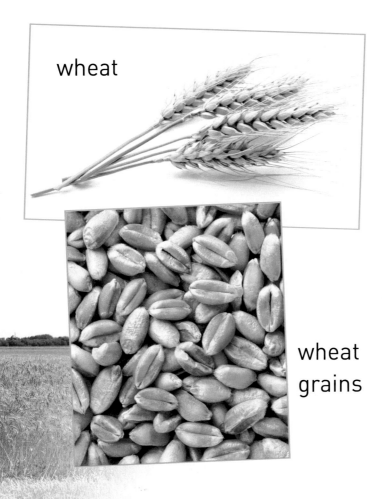

wheat

wheat
grains

Wheat is one crop that
many farmers grow.

Planting a crop

A wheat crop begins as **seeds**.

A farmer drives a **tractor** across the **field**.

The tractor pulls a **plow** that makes rows in the soil.

Then the tractor drives over the
field again, and drops seeds
into the rows.

The crop grows

Wheat seeds start to grow into green plants in the spring.

At the end of summer, the
wheat is golden yellow
and ready to be picked.

It is harvest time!

The combine at work

When it is time to harvest crops, every part of a combine harvester gets to work!

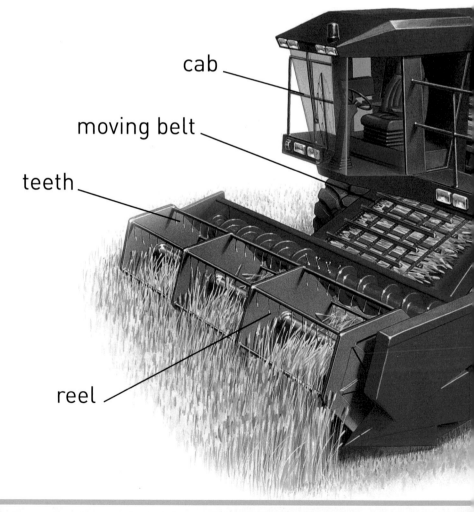

cab

moving belt

teeth

reel

See how many parts a combine harvester has!

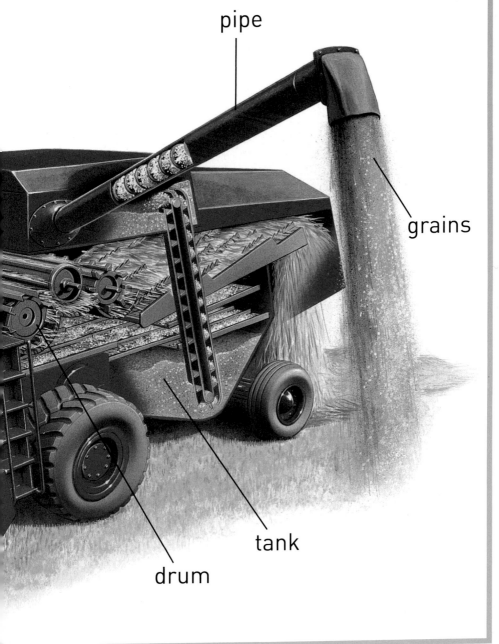

pipe

grains

tank

drum

Cutting the wheat

There are metal teeth on the reel of the combine harvester.

The teeth grab the wheat.

The reel pulls the wheat down to the cutter bar underneath it. The cutter bar is very sharp!

Two parts of wheat

The cut wheat moves to the drum.

The drum spins around and shakes the **stalks** of wheat.

The **grains** come off the stalks and fall into a tank.

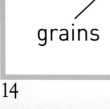

grains

Stalks without grains are called **straw**.

straw

drum

tank of grains

Grains

Grains pour out of a pipe
from the combine harvester
into a truck.

The truck goes to a **mill**.

At the mill, machines turn the grains into flour. We use this flour to make bread, pasta, and cakes.

Straw

Straw comes out of the
combine harvester
and falls to the ground.

A **baler** picks up
the straw.

The baler presses the straw
into **bales** and ties each bale
with string.

Farm animals sleep
on straw.

The driver

A combine harvester has a driver.
This is the driver's view of the field!

Sometimes a combine harvester works late into the night.

Every day, the driver checks and cleans the machine.

An important role

The combine harvester plays a very important role. It helps turn wheat into flour!

A tractor plows the field.

A tractor plants the seeds.

A combine harvester cuts the wheat.

A combine harvester separates the grains from the stalks.

A combine harvester pours the grains into a truck.

The truck takes the grains to a mill.

The mill turns the grains into flour.

Long ago

Before there were combine harvesters, all farmers had to harvest their crops by hand.

This took a very long time.

The first combine harvesters
were made about 200 years ago.
They were pulled by horses.

Next came
combine
harvesters
with engines!

More harvesting

Today, many farmers in poorer countries do not have combine harvesters and must cut their crops by hand.

Some combine harvesters
are used to harvest rice.

Rice grows in wet fields
in hot countries.

More harvesters

This is one of the largest combine harvesters in the world.

You can hold the smallest combine harvester with two hands!

Combine battle!

What can you do with a combine harvester that is too old to work?

You enter it in a farm machine contest!

The winning combine is the one that stays in one piece!

Glossary

bale a bundle of straw

baler a machine that presses straw into bales

crops plants grown on a farm for food

field a place where crops are planted

grains the seeds inside wheat

harvest to cut crops that are fully grown

mill a factory where machines turn grains into flour

plow a farm tool that cuts rows in the soil for planting seeds

seeds the parts of plants from which new plants can grow

stalks the stems of plants

straw wheat stalks without grains

tractor a farm machine that pulls heavy things